AF317020

A CHRIST-CENTERED MARRIAGE

A CHRIST-CENTERED MARRIAGE

FIONA STERLING

CONTENTS

CHAPTER 1

Introduction

In a world full of challenges and temptations, the only way to have a marriage that works and lasts is by doing it God's way. When Jesus explained the mystery of marriage to a group of teachers of religious law, he quoted from the book of Genesis, saying "Man shall leave his father and mother and the two become one." Marriage is not a man's idea, it is God's. There's no better way to have a strong, free, loving, faithful, Christlike, fruit-filled, Spirit-powered marriage than by basing it and centering it on the Lord Jesus Christ. After all, he said that he is the way.

All of our personal habits, communication patterns, attitudes, pet peeves, thoughts, and actions have the ability to either draw us closer to the Lord or separate us from him. They will also either draw us closer to each other or separate us from one another. The personal sanctification process grooms us into becoming a better reflection of the character of Christ and sets us free from the bondage that is sin. It enables us to love the Lord wholeheartedly by renewing our intimacy and fellowship with him, love others selflessly and determinedly, and love ourselves in a healthy, balanced, and constructive way. It is about the transformation of our characters into the image of Christ. The marriage sanctification process, which starts when two individuals come together to form a couple, is about working side-by-side and encouraging each other as we all continually go through this process, preserving, protecting, nurturing, investing, and growing together in unity, respect, order, joy, peace, perseverance, forgiveness, faith, and love. It is about becoming a better reflection of the Bridegroom with each day that goes by while continuing to have our curiosity, desires, zeal, and trust for him ongoingly renewed as well. Let's get our marriage right by doing it God's way as we develop an intimate and solid relationship with him.

Purpose of the Book

Many couples put little or no focus on the religious and spiritual part of their relationship, and it is our aim to restore the return of such vital focus there. We have strived to select articles that should be beneficial to everyone, regardless of your current marital status. This book is for you if you are single, engaged, married, living together and not married, separated, remarried, or divorced. While we will not tell you how to achieve physical attraction the world's way, we will offer up clear ideas for a marriage spiritual success that never grows old, spoils, or turns rancid. We have avoided blemished content offering commands and choices inferior to those found in the Holy Bible and have come to understand that leaving out Christ-centered relationships inspires the actions of human nature, the lowest denominator. This inspired us to only place our seal on what God created and Christ approves of.

This book is a collection of articles that we hope will provide Christian couples with invaluable support in their joint efforts to successfully build their marriage relationship. Our objective is to inspire you to make pleasing God, not self, the number one priority of your relationship. The question we want you to continuously search your personal conscience for an answer to is, "Is God well pleased with the way my spouse and I conduct our marriage?" We sincerely believe that a couple's sincere Christian devotion and obedience to God plays an essential role in creating a successful and enduring marriage. Consequently, we will remind you of this often by referencing numerous Bible scriptures that will foster and uplift your Christian faith. In so doing, we strive to create a very important balance in presenting information that holistically addresses issues in the religious, spiritual, and natural areas of life.

CHAPTER 2

Foundations of a Christ-centered Marriage

Putting Christ first is so important that in so many ways it becomes difficult to even imagine where we would be without our faith," said another couple. They were able to be open to the sacrament of marriage and said that Christ "is always present at our side, guiding us with His love." It had been Christ who had given them permission to evade "the darkness of sin and temptation to avoid it fully," said another pair, who stressed that "without our trust in God, we cannot believe we would have such a loving, trusting marriage united in our strong family that we now have if it were not by faith. This commitment to Christ and Our Lady means that they were there, giving them permission to build a relationship with a foundation of prayer as their "primary substantial form of interaction."

The 600 couples that participated in the study stressed that Christ was the foundation of their marriages. Christ has given "us the sense of purpose of our journey," wrote one couple. "Our roadmap guides everything we undertake as a spiritual journey," another paper. As a result, their commitment to and relationship with Christ has been reflected in their relationships with one another and with their children. Building their marriage life centered on the word of God builds "sites on secure land and survive the tempests; however, those who do not conform are like those who are swept away." As one couple put it: "When life gets tough, we now give it over to God in prayer and see how we can help one another like this. It has helped keep us comfortable." Others said of themselves, "Jesus has brought meaning and purpose in turbulent times to our marriage.

Understanding God's Design for Marriage
Understanding God's word brings understanding, meaning, and purpose into all aspects of life. Marriage is no exception. The Bible tells us the following statements about marriage:
- The creation of the woman in Genesis was to provide man with companionship. Genesis 2:18 states, "It is not good for the man to live alone. I will make a suitable companion to help him." As she was made from him, this is what Jesus said of the new creation in Matthew 19:5, "...will leave his father and guardian and will be united with his wife, and the two will become one." Notice the word "help", it does not mean servant, it means help or partner. - In Genesis 2:21-23, the woman was formed from part of the body of her husband. In the same way, the Church was born when Jesus was crucified. She was formed from the blood and water that flowed from her wounded side. This ceremony has the theological weight of baptism and nourishment as sacraments and is the source of love. - The Bible does not use the word trinity which outlines the concept or theology of the Holy Trinity from the beginning, but it affirms that there is one God, such as Paul's writings state in 2 Corinthians 13:14 "God of the Lord Jesus Christ, and the love of God". The famous biblical verse in Song of Solomon 2:1 is typical of the couple, in which the man says to his beloved, "I am the rose of Sharon and a lily of the valleys." The word "I" indicates the subject of contemplation,

the other, in dialogue with the different parts of the body, to make themselves known and to delight in them, and a symbol of this relationship with God. The couple, seeing the mysteries of God in their relationship, becomes one with the help of God. Since they became one during moments of ecstasy, this union is likened to the union with God, part of which is men. When properly looked at Christ is in the couple. When we have passed this look or love between us, we must constantly seek the love that exists as Trinity. When we have a genuine bond, this spirit will be present in our marriage.

Biblical Principles for a Strong Marriage

The husband-wife coequal model of marriage that the Bible demonstrates is completely different than what other philosophies state. Paul and the Apostle Peter each gave particular, clear, and relevant rules for moral Christian interactions between husbands and wives. Paul insisted on the oneness of husbands and wives in a similar way that Christ and Christians are depicted in the book of Ephesians... one body, one Spirit, one hope, one Lord, one faith, one baptism, and one God as well as Father of all, who is in us all, and works through us all.

The Bible is very clear on the Christian organization of marriage and family. It is our responsibility to represent Christ well because Christ does not wish for dysfunction to exist within our marriage. When we are able to serve our spouses by conquering sin in our hearts, we are demonstrating the power of the gospel. This is an opportunity to honor God and display His greatness by modeling Christianity to the world through our marriages. There will be difficulties, dissatisfaction, and differing desires in your relationship. As individuals, you are powerless to fix them or change individuals yourselves. It will require clashing with pride, loving someone who may not resemble you in personalities or interests, and giving away of oneself sacrificially. It will take consuming yourselves and your own personal pleasures and focusing on lifting up someone else. Christ-centeredness is a crucial measure in answering in love the biblical instruction for marriage.

CHAPTER 3

Communication in a Christ-centered Marriage

The Gospel of John has a beautiful example of what Christ, the Word made flesh, sounds like. It begins with John the Baptist, who is sitting with two of his disciples when he spots Jesus. He says to his disciples about Jesus, "Behold the Lamb of God!" With that one sentence, John the Baptist pointed Jesus out to his disciples, sent them to follow Jesus, and two of them become Jesus' first disciples. This is an example of how Jesus communicated through John the Baptist. With only that sentence spoken, Christ's word to the disciples was simple and direct. A good rule of thumb for Christian communication. When a husband or wife speaks to each other with truth, simplicity, love, and compassion, Christ is in their communication.

In any loving relationship, good, open, and honest communication is key to understanding and trust between partners. When two persons enter into the sacrament of marriage, the importance of communication between the husband and wife becomes even more evident. A Christ-centered marriage will have the living Word of God, Jesus Christ, as the foundation of the husband and wife's daily communicating. Communicating in a Christian marriage will develop a closer relationship between the husband and wife and God.

Effective Communication Skills

A Christ-centered marriage is built on a relationship with God, and on love for and commitment to each other. Proverbs 27:17 says, "As iron sharpens iron, so one man sharpens another." Your relationship with your partner will help to grow and develop you as a person; be open and honest with your partner for high compatibility and for spiritual as well as personal growth. Regular devotions, prayer, and communication help bring you to God and to each other. Develop your communication and your marriage now, and improve your relationship in these eight important areas: A healthy relationship provides a good measure of the compatibility of your personalities and gives you a basis for the development of an intimate relationship. Communication During the course of a marriage, both husband and wife are directly or indirectly involved in communication that is interpersonal, verbal, non-verbal, or physically and emotionally intimate. Consequently, for a strong, growing marital relationship, partners must communicate regularly and effectively.

This chapter provides two assessment tools that you and your partner can use to measure the compatibility of your love and marriage relationship, and to identify the specific areas where you need to improve your relationship. The third section contains articles on communication skills, and gives you practical instructions both on speaking and listening. You can evaluate your current level of listening and speaking skills by using the evaluation tool at the end of this section, and in turn develop a plan for improving areas that need further development.

Prayer and Communication

A child doesn't learn to walk without first having to crawl and cruise. In a like manner, infants don't learn how to talk without first listening to the sounds of the people around them. Communication is a very important aspect of the marriage. Don't play the guessing game; instead, learn to respect and listen to each other, and strive to improve in this aspect. There are many ways to improve, but one of the most important is to understand the other is trying to communicate. Start practicing active listening and empathy skills. Don't be so quick to respond; instead, listen to what the other is saying before formulating your thoughts. It's amazing how much you may be able to learn by just actively listening. And, show empathy when listening. You may be feeling a certain way after a long day at work, but by showing empathy when listening to the other, you are able to comfort the other emotionally. Be patient when showing empathy if you are unable to understand the other's feelings! This is a very important aspect of communication that can help the other feel secure in the relationship.

Prayer is a key part of helping your marriage grow to become what God wants. The Word of God (The Holy Bible) became one flesh with a woman named Mary and dwelt among us as "The Word became flesh and made His dwelling among us" (John 1:14). In a like way, the Word (Scripture) can become flesh in your marriage. If you exercise the graces promised through His Word, the Word will be made flesh again and again in your marriage and help it grow in ways you may not even understand. If you believe that God can perform miracles, why is it so difficult to believe what has been repeated throughout the history of the world? Why is it so difficult to trust in the power of prayer to change your world? If you're married, begin every morning by praying together to ask God for assistance. Attend church as frequently as possible to receive additional graces that can help grow and strengthen your marriage. Prayer can help your marriage grow in ways I can't begin to explain. The power is ready to be put to work in your relationship if you choose to accept and embrace it.

CHAPTER 4

Conflict Resolution and Forgiveness

Conflict Resolution and Forgiveness Two ingredients are crucial for resolving conflict between two people: asking for forgiveness and forgiving. When one person takes the initiative to ask for forgiveness regardless of who is in the wrong, the results are always positive. This sounds like a simple concept, but many marriages lack these two ingredients. If forgiving becomes an issue, you may want to see Seven Steps to Leading Forgiveness in a Relationship. Conflict and anger can bring about our deepest and strongest emotions. The level of frustration builds so great and yet we can't seem to resolve the problem. What can we do? Once we have honestly looked at our heart and are allowed to be unburdened and clean, that is when it becomes the easiest to forgive. Why? Because mercy isn't getting what we do deserve, and this brings love and unity. The expression "Mercy is not getting what you do deserve" is so true.

Introduction Is your marriage everything you wanted it to be? When two people become one family, friction is inevitable. This can lead to a troublesome marriage, but you can have a happy, peaceful home. Everyone wants a happy and loving relationship, but often we don't have the skills to make it happen. To have a Christ-centered marriage, it must be built by two people who are committed to changing and growing, with God's help. Our goal in this newsletter is to help you share a little bit about how God has worked in our lives to give us a wonderful marriage. If you're struggling with your marriage, or just looking for some helpful advice, then our monthly newsletters and hand-picked resources are for you. A Christ-centered marriage is based on three very important relationships: the husband's relationship with Christ, the wife's relationship with Christ, and then their personal, unique relationship with each other.

Dealing with Conflict Biblically

Conflicts must never be resolved by doing something that is morally wrong or sends a person into physical danger. However, settling an argument may require sacrifices. If one spouse is momentarily without love, the other spouse should forego their position for the moment and be patient. Flexibility and cooperation in confronting conflict are essential; hostility is unacceptable. It is important to remember that everything a person does in life must be done as a representative of their Savior and He did ask us to foster peace and help one another. With mutual love and respect, submission, communication, and application of biblical problem-solving principles, every couple can be confident of resolving tension in a way that is honoring to the Lord and beneficial to both the husband and wife.

No marriage is conflict free. Disagreement between a husband and wife is inevitable. In fact, it is a healthy sign in marriage. A marriage where a couple never disagrees can often mean that one or both of the spouses is not expressing their opinions and are choosing to avoid possible conflict. Nevertheless, couples are advised by the Lord to settle their disputes quickly. Giving room for anger and remaining unresolved is a place where the Devil can infiltrate. Unresolved tension can destroy marital intimacy. Only when couples deal with their anger and their respective emotions can they move to healing and be close and intimate again. Conflicts are opportunities for growth and closer emotional bonds. The Bible does not deny the existence of conflict; rather, it confronts it and instructs couples how to deal with it. In Matthew 18:15-17 we see conflict resolution as outlined by Jesus: 1) Approach your spouse directly concerning the matter; 2) Seek the counsel of a wise, impartial Christian if the conflict is unresolved; 3) Submit yourselves to the body of Christ, the church and let the elders counsel you in how to resolve your dispute. Paul also outlines how to resolve the dispute through in 1 Corinthians 6:1-8; there he instructs the saints not to bring their disputes before an unbeliever to resolve but to submit the matter to the saints to resolve.

The Power of Forgiveness

Forgiveness begins when we first recognize our pain, anger, betrayal, or frustration and take it to God. As we release our victimized emotions to God in prayer, we acknowledge the pain caused in our own lives and the effect it has on our behavior and spiritual walk. By faith, we exchange our wounds of rejection, unworthiness, insecurity, and anger for the love, acceptance, and security that comes from our relationship with God. The hurt is displaced by trust in God and the knowledge of His sustaining grace. The more we trust God and His healing process, the more completely the wounds of offense will heal. Using this process with our past wounds seals us as one in the bond of unity, thus allowing love to flow unhindered between our spouse and us.

Why is forgiveness so important? When forgiveness is released, so are the chains that bind us to the hurt from our pasts. This does not mean that the pain never existed or that we excuse the actions of the person who hurt us. We are not condoning the hurt or minimizing the loss by forgiving someone. Forgiveness does, however, unlock the door to our entrapment. It can set us free from unre-solved emotional turmoil, the torment of recurring flashbacks, and the constant gnawing of desire for vengeance. It releases us from being a prisoner to the tormentor and also prevents further hardening of our hearts. Forgiveness is a process with varying degrees. The deeper the pain, the deeper the process of forgiveness. Therefore, it is important to acknowledge each level of healing, making sure to work through each step to allow total forgiveness and complete emotional healing.

CHAPTER 5

Building Intimacy in Marriage

Intimacy cannot be conjured up at will. Although it is a built-in part of marriage, it cannot develop in an environment of suspicion, doubt, guilt, or anger. Intimacy can grow only where there is a climate of trust, understanding, cooperation, and love. When these attitudes exist, then the following factors become real tools for building and maintaining intimacy, a sense of we-ness, and unity in marriage. Factors which encourage the growth of marital intimacy are mutual respect, freedom from suspicion, trust, appreciation, cooperation, companionship in work and play, freedom to speak frankly, a spirit of equality, and a sense of humor. These factors are two sides of the same coin. They cannot be isolated, nor can they be expected to exist without some effort.

The preceding sections of this describe some aspects of intimacy in marriage. How we relate to one another is fundamental in building a strong marital bond. What we hope to have established is the need for husbands and wives to develop an abiding sense of unity, love, and trust so husband and wife can become "one flesh." In this part, we shall discuss characteristics of intimacy, factors which can help and hinder its development, and ways of maintaining intimacy once it has been achieved.

Physical Intimacy in a Godly Marriage

Sex in a godly marriage includes three key elements that fulfill the function of bonding the couple physically and emotionally. These are growth, caring attitudes, and oneness. Physical intimacy, in the context of marital love, is neither vulgar nor perverted. Sexual desire and needs are a wonderful experience given by God, so there's nothing wrong with feelings of physical attraction. In fact, they are a necessary part of God's plan for a lifelong marriage. It's how God created man and woman. In 1 Corinthians 7:7 it says that singleness is a gift, and in my heart of hearts, I believe it. God is love, and God created the bond of marriage. Sex is a beautiful part of physical love, and something He gave His many children to fulfill within the sanctity of marriage. However, Satan loves perverting things. Sort of like music is supposed to be used for praise of God, but he loves perverting it. Watch a few music videos and it becomes extremely obvious. However, as I mentioned before, it's not always going to be roses and candy. You will have times of conflict and disagreement in your marriage, but that's ok. Don't let Satan take advantage of that.

First, let me clarify something. There are some married couples who deprive each other of sexual fulfillment, which isn't right either. 1 Corinthians 7:2-5 says that "A man should fulfill his duty as a husband, and a woman should fulfill her duty as a wife..." and then goes on to say "The husband should not deprive his wife of sexual relations, and the wife should not deprive her husband, because doing this might come to temptations to Satan to tempt you. This is only a recommendation, not a command. But I wish everyone were like me. But God has given different gifts to different people. I have his gift of not marrying, and I also have his gift of serving him as he wants." There are people who feel called to be single, and there is nothing wrong with that. However, if you have gotten married, this passage goes on to say "...But I think that it is better for you to have desire to marry and to spend your lives together." So don't let Satan tempt you!

Emotional and Spiritual Intimacy

Couples need to be aware of the importance of feeling special in each other's eyes. God has brought two people together as physical, emotional, and spiritual companions for life. You must accept and appreciate the deep friendship God has given you. It is His will that we come to know Him, accept His love, and love others in return. Don't rush around God and your family and deliberately create the time and impetus to express your caring and love to your partner. Create an emotional, spiritual haven of love and acceptance together. Value your partner's physical, emotional, and spiritual well-being more than your own. Each partner must be willing to reveal personal feelings, weaknesses, and hurts to the other. Nothing destroys the emotional trust of a relationship like "contempt" - an attitude of never being able to do anything that is good enough.

One of the most distinctive features of emotional intimacy is sharing. At a deep level, communication is not just a matter of sharing facts or information. Sharing implies absorbing the pain of others into your life - to really care about what the other person is feeling. Mutual sharing is what will bring you and your spouse into close emotional intimacy. Your partner will come to understand your most private thoughts and feelings. Intimacy is making the other person feel very special, important, unique, and precious.

CHAPTER 6

Parenting in a Christ-centered Marriage

As Christian parents, we have many duties to fulfill. Every parent tells their children to look both ways when crossing the street. This rule applies to Christ and marriage. Human nature leads us to sin, and children are no different. When a dangerous or unsafe situation is evident, the natural tendency of children is to think they are invincible. They see the rule, but they don't really think it applies to them. "I have it under control, I will be careful." If, in fact, they did follow the rule, then rules would have no purpose. God has put boundaries in place, and he doesn't intend for them to be crossed. Rules protect us from evil, injury, and consequences. Without rules, trust, dreams, and possibly life would be lost. When our children sin, we need to address the problems as soon as we can. Once we see the sinful behavior, the consequences are almost always visible. We need to do our best to correct the sin and avoid any long-term damage.

The purpose of marriage is to bring two sinners together so they can help each other become more like Christ. It's important to understand what the ultimate goal is in a Christ-centered marriage. If God's goal is to make us more like Christ and Christ-likeness is the ultimate goal in life, everything outside our salvation should be to help us be more like our Savior. That would include marriage. Being Christ-centered doesn't stop at just marriage, but it includes everything in life that we aim to do. There is no question that Christ must be in every aspect of our life. In marriage, parenting is no different. Parenting in a Christ-centered marriage means that Christ is at the center of every decision and action that you make as a parent. There is really just one thing that the Lord requires of our children. Obey your parents in the Lord, for this is right. (Ephesians 6:1)

Raising Children with Christian Values

Christians will also be able to instill lessons of self-worth, true celebration of accomplishment, and acceptable code of conduct as Christians. Having a true Christian family enhances the strength and confidence of the parents as they are involved in the day to day encounters that help strengthen the marriage and family bond. Christian parents raise their children with a good understanding of God's laws and, by His grace, keep them. There are daily opportunities to provide examples and share the Word that applies to specific family situations. This knowledge and example affect the family and bring them together in a bond of love as they follow God's precepts. Plus, they look forward optimistically to the blessings of the future family that will sustain them.

When a couple is dedicated to raising their children in the Christian faith, it is sure to impact their marriage in countless ways. A Christ-centered marriage should have a God-centered family, and Christians have a great responsibility in ensuring that they nurture their children so they can grow into a relationship with Jesus. They start by leading the example, and then plant the seed of love, faith, hope, and compassion in their children. As they begin to nurture their spiritual relationship with God, the children will grow in favor with God and men and will naturally take to love, respect, and kindness in their everyday lives.

Unity in Parenting

You are the first role models that children see. A child, at a healthy developmental level, is usually malleable and automatically follows loud instructions and demands. If parents are in agreement and harmony as Christian role models, our future teens and adults are more likely to continue and follow them. Paired up privileges and consequences should mask any inconsistencies, so always make sure you have discussed your current issues with each other. Remember to complement each other and acknowledge each other's work on parenting. The loving bond you share must be balanced too. After the child is born, remember that you are not the first need but the first relationship that the child gets the opportunity to learn from. Quality husband and wife time has been proven to greatly affect the children and should be evaluated with your personal and family priorities.

Children flourish best in a stable, loving, and peaceful environment, so when they see both parents working together harmoniously on parenting and discipline, they are more likely to feel nurtured and safe. So, in Christ-like unity, there must be unity in the decisions made for parenting, like the types of food fed to the child. Play, prayer, and bonding time should always be in harmony. They should know their roles and not let any imbalance of work caused by adding kids. Unity, patience, and love should be the cornerstone of discipline too. Screaming, fighting, and the like obscenities is not the ideal way of solving or stopping a problem and usually results in added problems since it often promotes or enhances a behavior. They must find ways to provide discipline while building family unity and parental respect. There is strength in unity. The examples and rewards will be just. They alone are responsible for instilling not only the basics of respect but also for helping the children to become all that they can be.

CHAPTER 7

Navigating Challenges in Marriage

C hristians have less difficulty bowing their wills to God's; therefore they are better equipped to obey His commands, including the instructions given in Scripture for husbands and wives. Christ has etched a picture of the ultimate marriage in His covenant with the church, and by keeping that model in sight, couples will be trailblazers, leading their children as well as other believers. In doing so, Christians help harass a world that is lost in a quagmire of deceptive postmodern saturating marriage with ambiguity. Because the ultimate hope of resolving personality clashes and uniting divergent perspectives is possible in Christ, those couples who have Christ at the center of their marriage have good reason to express great joy and satisfaction.

When married, Christian couples hit the inevitable rough patches, it's important for them to realize how essential a Christ-centered marriage is in resolving problems, being a positive witness to others and fulfilling God's intention for His institution of marriage. Couples possessing a Christ-centered marriage are more effective in resolving conflicts because their perspective is clearer and focuses on the importance of their covenant to one another and to God.

Financial Struggles

Financial struggles are often common sources of stress and conflict in a marriage. Even though it seems that money is not directly related to Christianity, when we, as Christians, cannot handle our financial situations, the whole world's interpretation of poverty, misery, and hardship could potentially affect our ministry - the weak testimony of our financial ruin. The Bible teaches us that God is our Provider. Our Father knows what we need, and He wants to see us accept His provision. Wealth is His; money is only a medium of economic exchange. We must not love money. We have a responsibility to help others, especially our brothers in Christ who are in need. Nowadays, financial values are distorted. The world pursues wealth and material possessions. Whenever we become preoccupied with worldly possessions, worries mount and cause us to lower our guard. Satan tends to influence us to be proud and fret about our finances, and inability to handle these emotions effectively could potentially cause us to commit more sins and express symptoms of spiritual degeneration such as anxiety, indifference, and broken relationships. believes that couples need to agree on some basic financial principles that they are both comfortable with. They also have to remain true to their financial standing and communicate with each other on an ongoing basis concerning their decisions together. Absolute honesty, mutual respect, and being able to forgive are essential qualities in maintaining financial balance in a marriage. The seven tips in handling financial struggles are: Set Financial Goals, Be Contented, Live within Your Means, Communicate, Pray and Listen, always Seek Knowledge, tithe, and put God first, Renegotiate Payments and Other Alternatives, Plan for the Future, and have financial discussions.

Infidelity and Rebuilding Trust

Infidelity can have various forms. It could be physical - when you make love to someone who is not your spouse in the marriage covenant. It could be emotional - when anyone else's emotional needs get more priority than your spouse's. It could be through thoughts, words, or deeds. When we have constant interactions with someone else in such a way that we might be emotionally drawn to them, or feel as if we understand them in a way that our spouses do not, when outside influences lead to too much mental, physical, or emotional intimacy between you and your partner, involvement that would not be condoned between you and someone of the opposite sex, that may be the beginning of infidelity. But one point worthy of note is that the fact that you sometimes think that someone other than your spouse is attractive does not mean that you've started on a path to unfaithfulness. These thoughts are not so important as to when we start to justify them and in turn look forward to having them.

Infidelity can be a painful and devastating experience, one we hope to avoid at all costs. However, it's one of those things that happen in this world - it's rampant, and there's no denying that. And knowing that God loves us so much, that He always wants the best for us, He has set up rules for us that would help to ensure that we're not led on the wrong track by the many temptations that abound. Infidelity is just an avenue for Satan to attack marriages which have already drifted from God's way. When we disobey God's good commands, it comes with some consequences that will not be too funny for us. But with God's help, even when these consequences come our way, we will find grace to cope and conquer. In our quest to obey God, to please Him in our marriages, not being unfaithful to our spouses should be the very first step.

CHAPTER 8

Maintaining a Strong Relationship with God

To continue God's presence in our lives as a couple, we need to maintain our own individual relationships with God. Some tips that we find helpful are:

1. Time in scripture: Just as the Good Book says, we need to be mindful of what God is telling us. As a physical object, a Bible can be a great reminder of God's impact on our lives.

2. Help from an outside source: There are many devotional books at our disposal. Listening to a preacher or reading spiritual material can add religion to our lives, which ultimately helps in creating a strong faith together. Simply filling our senses with positive, Christian messages is helpful and certainly available.

3. Prayer is a good method for keeping open the channel of divine communication. Remember to pray for God to send help to strengthen us in the areas of our lives where He determines that we each need it, and we will receive grace from Him.

4. Service work: Without doing physical things to help others, we will find a lack of spiritual direction. As Christian spouses, continuing to do service will bring new insights to life that can be passed on by mutually searching for the correct meanings.

5. Remembering how one came to have fellowship with God and repeating those steps can restore our relationship to God. If we ask what God wants us to do in a situation where we feel that we are not close to Him and then act upon those ideas, it can spur a renewal in both of our spiritual directions.

Individual Spiritual Growth

In order for each member of a couple to grow individually, there are any number of approaches that can work. The one caution is that each member should expect to travel his or her own path. Each person's relationship with the Lord is unique to that person. Our Lord loves to spend personal time with each of us. While there is great value in prayer and worship as a couple - daily reading of scripture or devotionals - there is also great value in a personal connection to the Lord. After all, God created us uniquely in order that we might enjoy the variety of His creation. Each person's relationship with the Lord is something that is personal, and as such is likely to change based to some extent on life's circumstances. The things of life are often designed to help us grow, and so will affect our relationship with the Lord. The things that we find most meaningful are often linked more to closure time with Him. It is not always reflective of what others might think ought to be meaningful to us.

It has often been said that in order to have a strong marriage, each of the individuals involved must be very strong in his or her own right. This is particularly true in spiritually-based marriages. The skills and tools of the previous section are all necessary in order to strengthen and build the relationship. Each of these, however, is an outward aid in developing the relationship. How strong the relationship itself can become is very limited if the individuals involved are not strong - both in general and spiritually. The discussion back in chapter three linked spiritual strength and wisdom to a strong marriage. From a Christian point of view, there is no question that the closer one is to Christ, the greater the support, and the more unity can be found in the marriage itself.

Spiritual Practices as a Couple

Before a couple undertakes combining fasting and prayer practices, they must be honest with each other, honestly seeking the Lord as to how as a couple they should proceed. Concerning the couple specifically, what is the intent of their fasting? What shared vision or focus do they believe God has for them as a couple? What do they invite God to teach and work within them? Only God gives clarification. Each person needs to be convinced individually and then corporately as to what they are committing themselves to. Can both commit to their agreed-upon fast square before the Lord? Ensure that the request comes from a humble and contrite heart. Entering into fasting with selfish intent can lead to outright condemnation. It is important for the couple to remain pure before the Lord throughout the entire process – in focus, concentration, dedication, and diet – allowing God to have complete reign in their lives.

Prayer and fasting are both personal, spiritual disciplines. They are intended to help individuals focus their attention on God, seeking intimacy with and direction from Him. As married individuals, partaking in prayer and fasting also deepens and reforges the marital bond. While it certainly is important that each husband and wife spend time in prayer and fasting as individuals, periodically gathering as a couple to do these things – even weekly – energizes unity and enhances the couple's common life. Through this process, husbands and wives selflessly patronize and support each other as we offer our entire beings in faithfulness and devotion to the Lord.

CHAPTER 9

Conclusion

All said, the best planning in the world can't guarantee a successful marriage. But if you're marrying on faith, hope, and love, well, to quote God again, "What more could I have done for my vine?" In marriage, a Christ-centered marriage, we realize that the true essence of love is: "This is my commandment, that you love one another as I have loved you. There is no greater love than to lay down one's life for his friends." God's way of life works! God's living blueprint for happy marriages is available to you and your loved ones. Please consider it!

If you have a Christ-centered marriage, you have the best and true foundation for wedded bliss. But please, won't you remember, my dear sisters and brothers, that God's love and guidance are the supports which are woven throughout the mesh of our married lives. Often, while planning a Christian wedding, the importance of a Christ-centered marriage is forgotten. While there's plenty of helpful hints, practical tips, and marriage advice, newlywed assistance designed to solve the typical war zone stress of overspending and overemphasizing on the societal day of marriage, little is available to remind budding brides about the consequences of not inviting Christ.

Reflecting on the Journey

Christian marriage is life's greatest sacrament. Your marriage works well when you are faithful to your baptismal commitments and live your Christian faith. That is why this personal reflection is such an important part of your marriage. Part of the journey is recognizing that marriage is a call to grow in holiness together, to become a clear sign of someone who is in a living relationship with the living God. Marriage is your choice to love someone really well. As one of our favorite priests at our church always tells us, "marriage is when God asks us to borrow each other for a certain amount of time, to borrow Him, and bring the other person to Him." It is such a beautiful calling that was first instituted by God from the very beginning of the universe. So what does that mean for you? It means that as a Christian couple in love, Jesus is here waiting for you in your journey towards a holy marriage.

Hooray! You have made it to the end of this incredible journey of diving into God's plan for your relationship. What a journey it has been. We started with basic reflections to a deeper understanding of how your life and career paths lead you to each other. We talked about having a God-centered relationship. Now, with the end in sight, we reflect at the core of our journey: Jesus, the Heart of our marriage. In your marriage, Jesus should always be on the forefront of your thoughts, words, and actions. No matter where the journey of your marriage takes you, Jesus will be there waiting for you, loving you, and helping you both grow, regardless of what life throws at you.